Interview Guide for Software Testing and Quality Assurance.

80 Questions and Answers

Julia Portley

Welcome to "80 Interview Questions for Software Testing and Quality Assurance." This book is designed to serve as a comprehensive guide for both job seekers and hiring managers in the field of software testing and quality assurance. Whether you are a seasoned professional looking to sharpen your interview skills or a newcomer preparing for your first job interview, this book offers a wealth of valuable insights and practical advice to help you succeed.

In today's competitive job market, it's essential to be well-prepared and confident when facing interviews. This book covers a wide range of topics, including software testing principles, methodologies, techniques, tools, and best practices. Each question is carefully crafted to assess your knowledge, skills, and experience in software testing and quality assurance, allowing you to showcase your expertise and stand out from the competition.

For hiring managers and recruiters, this book serves as a valuable resource for identifying top talent and evaluating candidates' suitability for software testing roles. The questions provided are designed to probe candidates' understanding of key concepts, their problem-solving abilities, and their ability to think critically and analytically in real-world testing scenarios.

Whether you're a job seeker or a hiring manager, "80 Interview Questions for Software Testing and Quality Assurance" is your go-to resource for mastering the interview process and making informed hiring decisions. Let's embark on this journey together and unlock the secrets to success in software testing and quality assurance interviews!

0.5. Question: What is software testing, and why is it important?

Answer: Software testing is a process aimed at evaluating the functionality and performance of a software application to ensure it meets specified requirements and quality standards. It involves executing the software under controlled conditions and comparing actual results with expected outcomes to identify defects or discrepancies. Software testing is crucial because it helps detect and rectify defects early in the development lifecycle, reducing the risk of software failures, enhancing reliability, and improving user satisfaction.

1. **Question: What are the different types of software testing?**

    Answer: There are several types of software testing, each serving a specific purpose in the software development lifecycle:
    - Unit Testing: Testing individual components or modules of the software in isolation to verify their functionality.
    - Integration Testing: Testing the interaction between integrated components to ensure they work together as expected.
    - System Testing: Testing the entire system as a whole to validate its compliance with specified requirements and user expectations.
    - Acceptance Testing: Testing conducted to determine whether the software meets the acceptance criteria and is ready for deployment.
    - Regression Testing: Testing performed to ensure that recent changes or enhancements to the software do not adversely affect existing functionality.
    - Performance Testing: Testing the performance characteristics of the software, such as responsiveness, scalability, and resource utilization, under various conditions.
    - Security Testing: Testing conducted to identify vulnerabilities and security flaws in the software to protect it from potential threats and breaches.
    - Usability Testing: Testing the user-friendliness and ease of use of the software to ensure a positive user experience.
    - Compatibility Testing: Testing the software's compatibility with different operating systems, devices, browsers, and environments to ensure consistent performance across platforms.

- Exploratory Testing: Testing conducted without predefined test cases to explore the software's behaviour and uncover defects through real-time exploration and experimentation.
-

2. **Question: Can you explain the difference between functional and non-functional testing?**

   Answer: Functional testing focuses on verifying the functional requirements and behaviour of the software, such as user interactions, data processing, and system functionality. It ensures that the software performs its intended functions correctly according to specified requirements. Non-functional testing, on the other hand, evaluates the non-functional aspects of the software, such as performance, reliability, usability, security, and compatibility. It assesses the software's quality attributes and characteristics beyond its basic functionality to ensure it meets user expectations and performance standards.

3. **Question: What is a test plan, and what information does it include?**

   Answer: A test plan is a comprehensive document that outlines the approach, scope, objectives, resources, schedule, and deliverables of the testing process for a software project. It serves as a roadmap for the testing activities and provides guidance to the testing team on how to proceed with testing. A test plan typically includes the following information:
   - Introduction: Overview of the software project, objectives, and scope of testing.
   - Test Strategy: Approach and methodologies used for testing, including types of testing, tools, and techniques.
   - Test Scope: In-scope and out-of-scope items, features, and functionalities to be tested.
   - Test Environment: Hardware, software, tools, and resources required for testing.
   - Test Deliverables: List of documents, reports, and artifacts to be produced as part of the testing process.
   - Test Schedule: Timeline, milestones, and dependencies for the testing activities.
   - Roles and Responsibilities: Roles, responsibilities, and assignments of team members involved in testing.

- Risks and Assumptions: Potential risks, assumptions, and constraints affecting the testing process.
- Exit Criteria: Criteria for determining when testing is complete and the software is ready for release.
- Approvals: Sign-off and approval process for the test plan by stakeholders and project sponsors.
-

4. **Question: How do you prioritize test cases for execution?**

   Answer: Test case prioritization involves identifying and categorizing test cases based on factors such as criticality, risk, complexity, dependencies, and business impact. Test cases that cover critical functionalities, high-risk areas, and frequently used features are prioritized for execution to ensure maximum test coverage within time and resource constraints. Priority levels such as high, medium, and low are assigned to test cases based on their importance and relevance to the testing objectives. Test cases are executed in the order of priority, starting with high-priority test cases, followed by medium and low-priority ones, to focus testing efforts on the most critical areas and maximize the effectiveness of testing.

5. **Question: What is the difference between black-box testing and white-box testing?**

   Answer: Black-box testing, and white-box testing are two complementary approaches to software testing that focus on different aspects of the software:
   - Black-box testing, also known as behavioural testing, involves testing the functionality of the software from an external or end-user perspective without knowledge of its internal structure, design, or implementation details. Testers interact with the software interface or user interface to validate its inputs, outputs, and behaviour against specified requirements. Black box testing techniques include equivalence partitioning, boundary value analysis, decision tables, and state transition testing.
   - White-box testing, also known as structural testing or glass-box testing, involves testing the internal structure, logic, and code of the software to ensure its correctness, completeness, and efficiency. Testers have access to the source code and use knowledge of the software's architecture, design, and

implementation to design test cases that exercise different paths, branches, and conditions within the code. White-box testing techniques include statement coverage, branch coverage, path coverage, and condition coverage.

6. **Question: How do you identify and report software defects?**

   Answer: Identifying and reporting software defects is a critical aspect of the testing process, and it involves the following steps:
   - Defect Identification: Testers use various testing techniques such as manual testing, automated testing, exploratory testing, and user feedback to identify defects or discrepancies in the software. They execute test cases, observe the software's behaviour, and compare actual results with expected outcomes to identify deviations, errors, or anomalies.
   - Defect Logging: Testers document defects in a defect tracking system or bug tracking tool with detailed information such as defect description, steps to reproduce, environment details, severity, priority, and screenshots or attachments. They provide clear and concise descriptions of the observed behaviour, expected behaviour, and impact of the defect on the software's functionality, performance, or usability.
   - Defect Prioritization: Testers prioritize defects based on factors such as severity, impact, frequency, business impact, and customer or user feedback. Critical or high-priority defects that affect essential functionality, security, or user experience are prioritized for immediate resolution, while lower-priority defects may be deferred or addressed in subsequent releases.
   - Defect Reporting: Testers communicate defects to relevant stakeholders, including developers, project managers, and quality assurance team members, using standardized defect reports or defect management tools. They provide clear and actionable information about each defect, including its status, assigned owner, resolution timeline, and any dependencies or related defects. They also track and monitor the status of defects throughout the defect lifecycle, from identification to resolution, to ensure timely closure and validation.

7. **Question: What is the purpose of regression testing, and when should it be performed?**

Answer: Regression testing is a type of software testing that verifies that recent changes or enhancements to the software do not adversely affect existing functionality or introduce new defects. It ensures that the software continues to perform as intended after modifications, updates, or fixes are made. Regression testing should be performed whenever there are changes to the software, such as bug fixes, patches, enhancements, or new feature implementations. It is typically executed as part of the software release cycle or development process, after each iteration, sprint, or change to the codebase, to validate the stability and integrity of the software across releases and iterations.

8. **Question: Can you explain the concept of test-driven development (TDD)?**

   Answer: Test-driven development (TDD) is a software development approach where tests are written before the code is implemented. It follows a cycle of writing tests, writing code to make the tests pass, and refactoring the code to improve its design and maintainability. In TDD, developers write automated unit tests based on the expected behaviour of the software, focusing on specific requirements or features. They then write the minimal amount of code necessary to make the tests pass, ensuring that the code meets the specified requirements and behaves as expected. TDD promotes code quality, test coverage, and design clarity by encouraging developers to write modular, testable, and maintainable code from the outset.

9. **Question: How do you ensure that software testing is thorough and comprehensive?**

   Answer: Thorough and comprehensive software testing requires a systematic and disciplined approach, encompassing various testing techniques, methodologies, and best practices. It involves the following key strategies:
   - Requirement Analysis: Understanding and analysing the software requirements to identify testable features, functions, and behaviours, and define clear, concise test objectives and success criteria.
   - Test Planning: Developing a detailed test plan that outlines the scope, approach, resources, schedule, and deliverables of the

testing process, and defines test strategies, techniques, and methodologies to be employed.
- Test Case Design: Creating comprehensive test cases that cover various scenarios, conditions, and use cases, ensuring adequate test coverage across all functional and non-functional requirements.
- Test Execution: Executing test cases systematically and methodically to validate the software against specified requirements, verifying functionality, performance, security, usability, and other quality attributes.
- Defect Management: Identifying, logging, prioritizing, and tracking defects throughout the testing process, ensuring timely resolution and validation to maintain software quality and stability.
- Test Automation: Automating repetitive and time-consuming testing tasks using test automation tools and frameworks to improve efficiency, reliability, and repeatability of testing, and accelerate the testing process.
- Continuous Improvement: Iteratively evaluating and refining testing processes, methodologies, and techniques based on lessons learned, feedback, and evolving project requirements, to enhance the effectiveness and efficiency of software testing over time.

10. **Question: Can you explain the difference between smoke testing and sanity testing?**

Answer: Smoke testing and sanity testing are both types of preliminary testing performed to ensure the stability and readiness of the software for further testing. However, they serve different purposes and target different aspects of the software:
- Smoke Testing: Smoke testing, also known as build verification testing, is a type of non-exhaustive testing aimed at quickly verifying whether the critical functionalities of the software work correctly after a new build or release. It focuses on validating basic functionalities and essential features to determine if the software build is stable enough for further testing. Smoke tests are typically automated and cover high-priority test cases representing core functionalities to identify showstopper defects early in the testing process.

- Sanity Testing: Sanity testing, also known as subset testing or build acceptance testing, is a type of focused testing aimed at quickly verifying whether specific changes or enhancements to the software have been implemented correctly and have not introduced any major defects or regressions. It focuses on validating specific functionalities or areas of the software affected by recent changes to ensure they behave as expected and do not impact existing functionality. Sanity tests are typically performed manually and cover critical test cases representing recently modified features or areas of the software to ensure their stability and integrity before further testing.

In summary, while both smoke testing and sanity testing are preliminary testing techniques used to assess the stability and readiness of the software, smoke testing verifies the overall build stability and readiness for testing, while sanity testing validates specific changes or enhancements made to the software to ensure their correctness and integrity.

12. **Question:** What is the difference between verification and validation in software testing?

Answer: Verification ensures that the software meets its specified requirements and adheres to predefined standards and guidelines. It focuses on evaluating the work products (such as requirements, design, and code) to ensure they are correct and complete. Validation, on the other hand, ensures that the software meets user needs and expectations and performs its intended functions correctly. It focuses on evaluating the software itself to determine if it meets user requirements and delivers the desired outcomes.

13. **Question:** What is a test case, and what information should it include?

Answer: A test case is a detailed document that describes a specific test scenario, including inputs, actions, expected outcomes, and execution conditions. It serves as a blueprint for executing the test and verifying the software's behaviour. A test case should include the following information:
- Test case ID and title
- Test objective or purpose

- Preconditions and test environment setup
- Test inputs or data
- Test steps or actions to be performed
- Expected results or outcomes
- Actual results (for execution and verification)
- Pass/fail criteria
- Test status and comments

14. **Question: How do you ensure that test cases cover all requirements?**

Answer: Ensuring test coverage requires a systematic approach to test case design and prioritization. Techniques such as requirement traceability matrix (RTM), equivalence partitioning, boundary value analysis, and decision tables can help ensure comprehensive test coverage by mapping test cases to specific requirements, functionalities, and user scenarios. Additionally, cross-functional collaboration with stakeholders, developers, and business analysts can help identify and prioritize test cases based on criticality, risk, and business impact to ensure maximum coverage of requirements.

15. **Question: What is a defect life cycle, and how do you manage defects throughout the life cycle?**

Answer: The defect life cycle describes the stages through which a defect progresses from identification to resolution. It typically includes stages such as New, Assigned, Open, In Progress, Fixed, Verified, and Closed. Defects are logged, tracked, and managed using a defect tracking system or bug tracking tool, where they are assigned to appropriate stakeholders (such as developers, testers, or project managers) for resolution. Defects undergo triage, prioritization, assignment, resolution, verification, and closure based on severity, priority, status, and resolution timeline to ensure timely resolution and quality assurance.

16. **Question: How do you conduct regression testing efficiently?**

Answer: Regression testing can be conducted efficiently using various strategies and techniques:

- Prioritize test cases based on criticality, risk, and impact to focus testing efforts on high-risk areas and essential functionalities.
- Automate repetitive and time-consuming test cases using test automation tools and frameworks to accelerate testing and increase coverage.
- Implement version control and baseline management to track changes, identify impacted areas, and selectively execute relevant test cases.
- Use techniques such as selective regression testing, impact analysis, and risk-based testing to identify and prioritize test cases for regression testing based on recent changes and their potential impact on existing functionality.
- Adopt continuous integration and continuous delivery (CI/CD) practices to automate build, test, and deployment processes and ensure timely execution of regression tests as part of the software delivery pipeline.
-

17. Question: What is exploratory testing, and when is it used?

Answer: Exploratory testing is a manual testing technique where testers explore the software, experiment with its features, and design test cases on-the-fly based on their intuition, experience, and domain knowledge. It involves simultaneous test design, execution, and learning to uncover defects, scenarios, and user experiences not covered by predefined test cases. Exploratory testing is used in dynamic and uncertain environments, such as agile development, ad-hoc testing, usability testing, and user acceptance testing, to complement scripted testing and uncover unexpected behaviours, edge cases, and usability issues.

18. Question: How do you measure the effectiveness of your testing efforts?

Answer: Measuring the effectiveness of testing efforts requires defining relevant metrics, collecting data, and analysing key performance indicators (KPIs) to evaluate testing progress, quality, and efficiency. Common metrics for measuring testing effectiveness include:
- Test coverage: Percentage of requirements, functionalities, or code covered by test cases.
- Defect density: Number of defects identified per unit of code, test case, or project.

- Defect detection rate: Rate at which defects are identified and resolved during testing.
- Test execution progress: Percentage of test cases executed, passed, failed, or pending.
- Test efficiency: Ratio of passed tests to total tests executed, indicating the effectiveness of testing efforts.
- Test cycle time: Time taken to execute test cycles or iterations, from planning to closure.
- Test effectiveness ratio: Ratio of detected defects to total defects, indicating the effectiveness of testing in identifying defects.
- Customer satisfaction: Feedback from stakeholders, users, and customers on the quality and usability of the software.

19. **Question: What is the difference between static testing and dynamic testing?**

Answer: Static testing and dynamic testing are two complementary approaches to software testing that focus on different aspects of the software:
- Static Testing: Static testing is a verification technique that evaluates the software without executing the code. It includes techniques such as code reviews, walkthroughs, inspections, and static analysis to identify defects, errors, and inconsistencies in the software artifacts (such as requirements, design, and code) early in the development lifecycle.
- Dynamic Testing: Dynamic testing is a validation technique that evaluates the software by executing the code and observing its behaviour. It includes techniques such as functional testing, integration testing, system testing, and acceptance testing to validate the software against specified requirements and user expectations and identify defects or deviations in its behaviour during execution.

In summary, while static testing focuses on analysing software artifacts statically without execution, dynamic testing involves executing the software dynamically to validate its behaviour and functionality.

20. **Question: How do you ensure that your testing process is aligned with Agile development practices?**

Answer: Ensuring alignment with Agile development practices requires adopting Agile testing principles, techniques, and methodologies that emphasize collaboration, flexibility, and responsiveness. Key strategies for aligning testing with Agile development include:
- Embracing iterative and incremental testing: Conducting testing in short, focused iterations or sprints to validate functionality, gather feedback, and adapt testing strategies based on changing requirements and priorities.
- Collaborating closely with cross-functional teams: Engaging with stakeholders, developers, product owners, and other team members throughout the development lifecycle to clarify requirements, define acceptance criteria, and prioritize testing activities effectively.
- Implementing test automation: Automating testing tasks, including unit testing, integration testing, and regression testing, to accelerate testing, increase coverage, and support continuous integration and delivery (CI/CD) practices.
- Leveraging Agile testing frameworks: Adopting Agile testing frameworks such as Scrum, Kanban, and Extreme Programming (XP) to streamline testing processes, optimize resource utilization, and ensure transparency, collaboration, and alignment with Agile principles.
- Adapting test planning and execution: Iteratively planning, designing, and executing test cases based on user stories, acceptance criteria, and sprint goals to validate incremental changes, gather feedback, and ensure the quality and stability of the software throughout the development lifecycle.

21. **Question:** What is the difference between equivalence partitioning and boundary value analysis?

Answer: Equivalence partitioning and boundary value analysis are both test case design techniques used to identify test cases based on input conditions, but they focus on different aspects:
- Equivalence Partitioning: Equivalence partitioning divides the input domain of a software component into equivalence classes, where each class represents a set of equivalent input values that should produce the same result. Test cases are then selected from each equivalence class to ensure comprehensive coverage of the input space while avoiding redundancy.

- Boundary Value Analysis: Boundary value analysis focuses on identifying test cases at the boundaries of equivalence classes, as boundary values are more likely to reveal defects than values within the range. Test cases are designed to test the minimum and maximum values, as well as values just above and below the boundaries, to verify the software's behaviour near critical points.

22. Question: How do you approach testing for mobile applications?

Answer: Testing mobile applications requires a comprehensive approach that considers various factors such as device diversity, platform fragmentation, network conditions, and user experience. Key aspects of testing mobile applications include:
- Platform compatibility testing: Testing the application on different devices, operating systems, and screen sizes to ensure compatibility and consistency across platforms.
- User interface testing: Evaluating the usability, navigation, layout, and responsiveness of the application on mobile devices to ensure a seamless user experience.
- Performance testing: Assessing the application's performance under different network conditions, load levels, and device configurations to ensure responsiveness, speed, and reliability.
- Security testing: Identifying and mitigating security vulnerabilities such as data breaches, unauthorized access, and malware threats to protect sensitive information and ensure user privacy.
- Device-specific testing: Testing device-specific features such as GPS, camera, accelerometer, and touch gestures to ensure functionality and integration with device hardware and sensors.
- Network testing: Evaluating the application's behaviour under different network conditions, including varying bandwidth, latency, and connectivity, to ensure robustness and resilience in real-world scenarios.

23. Question: What are the advantages of automated testing, and when is it beneficial?

Answer: Automated testing offers several advantages over manual testing, including:

- Faster execution: Automated tests can be executed much faster than manual tests, allowing for quicker feedback and faster release cycles.
- Increased coverage: Automated tests can cover a wider range of scenarios, configurations, and data sets than manual tests, leading to better test coverage and defect detection.
- Consistency: Automated tests perform the same steps consistently each time they are executed, reducing the risk of human error and ensuring repeatability and reliability of test results.
- Reusability: Automated tests can be reused across different projects, releases, and environments, saving time and effort in test development and maintenance.
- Regression testing: Automated tests are well-suited for regression testing, allowing for quick and efficient validation of existing functionality after changes or updates to the software.

Automated testing is beneficial when:
- Tests need to be executed repeatedly, such as regression testing or smoke testing.
- Tests involve complex or repetitive tasks that are prone to human error.
- Tests require rapid feedback and continuous integration, such as in Agile or DevOps environments.
- Tests need to be executed across multiple configurations, platforms, or environments.

24. Question: What is a test management tool, and how does it help in software testing?

Answer: A test management tool is a software application used to manage and organize the testing process, including test planning, design, execution, and reporting. It provides features such as test case management, requirement traceability, test execution tracking, defect management, and reporting capabilities. Test management tools help streamline testing activities, improve collaboration among team members, and ensure transparency, consistency, and traceability in the testing process. They facilitate efficient test planning, execution, and analysis, allowing testers to manage test assets, track test progress, and generate test reports to communicate testing status and results to stakeholders effectively.

25. Question: Can you explain the difference between positive testing and negative testing?

Answer: Positive testing and negative testing are two approaches to software testing that focus on different aspects of system behaviour:
- Positive Testing: Positive testing verifies that the software behaves as expected when provided with valid inputs and conditions. It validates the correct functionality of the software by testing positive scenarios, where inputs are within the expected range, conditions are met, and the software should produce the desired outcomes. Positive testing ensures that the software handles valid data, user interactions, and system responses correctly without errors or exceptions.
- Negative Testing: Negative testing, also known as error or failure testing, validates the software's behaviour under invalid or unexpected inputs and conditions. It tests negative scenarios, where inputs are outside the expected range, conditions are violated, or the software encounters abnormal or erroneous conditions. Negative testing aims to uncover defects, vulnerabilities, and weaknesses in the software by testing error-handling mechanisms, boundary conditions, and edge cases that may lead to unexpected behaviours, crashes, or security breaches.

26. Question: How do you determine the test coverage for a software application?

Answer: Test coverage refers to the extent to which the software has been tested and the degree to which various aspects of the software have been exercised by test cases. Test coverage can be determined using different techniques and metrics, including:
- Requirements coverage: Assessing the percentage of requirements or user stories covered by test cases to ensure that all functional and non-functional requirements are tested.
- Code coverage: Measuring the percentage of code executed by test cases to ensure that all statements, branches, and paths in the code are exercised during testing.
- Functional coverage: Evaluating the coverage of different functional areas, features, and use cases of the software to ensure comprehensive testing of all functionalities and user interactions.

- Risk-based coverage: Prioritizing test cases based on risk factors such as criticality, complexity, and impact to focus testing efforts on high-risk areas and ensure maximum coverage of potential defects.

Test coverage analysis involves identifying gaps, redundancies, and overlaps in test coverage and iteratively refining test plans, test cases, and test suites to achieve optimal coverage and ensure the quality and reliability of the software.

27. Question: What is load testing, and why is it important?

Answer: Load testing is a type of performance testing that evaluates the software's behaviour under varying levels of load, stress, and concurrency to assess its performance, scalability, and reliability under real-world conditions. Load testing simulates multiple users, transactions, or requests accessing the software simultaneously to measure its response time, throughput, resource utilization, and stability under peak loads. Load testing helps identify performance bottlenecks, capacity limits, and scalability issues early in the development lifecycle, allowing organizations to optimize resource allocation, infrastructure provisioning, and system design to meet user demands and performance expectations.

28. Question: How do you prioritize defects for resolution?

Answer: Prioritizing defects for resolution involves assessing the severity, impact, and urgency of each defect and prioritizing them based on their potential risk to the project and users. Common factors considered when prioritizing defects include:
- Severity: The impact of the defect on the software's functionality, usability, performance, security, or compliance. Defects with higher severity levels, such as critical or showstopper defects, are typically prioritized for immediate resolution.
- Impact: The extent to which the defect affects the user experience, business operations, or system functionality. Defects with a significant impact on critical features or user workflows are prioritized higher than those with minimal impact.
- Reproducibility: The frequency and consistency with which the defect occurs or can be reproduced. Defects that are reproducible

or occur frequently are prioritized higher than those that are sporadic or intermittent.
- Customer feedback: Feedback from stakeholders, users, or customers regarding the importance, urgency, or business impact of the defect. Defects that align with user priorities or business goals are prioritized accordingly.
- Business impact: The potential financial, operational, or reputational consequences of the defect to the organization or project. Defects that pose significant risks or liabilities are prioritized for immediate resolution to mitigate potential adverse effects.

29.Question: What is API testing, and why is it important?

Answer: API (Application Programming Interface) testing is a type of software testing that focuses on verifying the functionality, performance, and reliability of application programming interfaces used to communicate and exchange data between different software components, systems, or services. API testing validates the behavior of APIs by sending requests, receiving responses, and verifying the data, parameters, and interactions according to specified requirements and expectations. API testing is important for several reasons:

- Ensuring interoperability: API testing verifies that APIs interact correctly with other software components, systems, or services, ensuring interoperability and compatibility across different platforms, technologies, and environments.
- Validating integration: API testing validates the integration and communication between software modules, services, or applications, ensuring seamless data exchange and interoperability between systems.
- Detecting defects early: API testing helps identify defects, errors, and inconsistencies in the software architecture, data flow, and communication protocols early in the development lifecycle, enabling timely resolution and preventing downstream impacts.
- Supporting automation: API testing can be automated using tools and frameworks to accelerate testing, increase coverage, and support continuous integration and delivery (CI/CD) practices, improving efficiency, reliability, and repeatability of testing.
- Enhancing security: API testing helps identify security vulnerabilities, such as unauthorized access, data breaches, or

injection attacks, by validating authentication, authorization, encryption, and data integrity mechanisms implemented in the API.

30. Question: How do you handle test data management and test environment setup?

Answer: Test data management and test environment setup are critical aspects of software testing that require careful planning, preparation, and maintenance. Key strategies for handling test data management and test environment setup include:

- Test data identification: Identifying and selecting appropriate test data sets that represent realistic scenarios, conditions, and use cases to ensure comprehensive test coverage and effective defect detection.
- Test data generation: Generating synthetic or anonymized test data using tools, scripts, or data masking techniques to create realistic test scenarios and protect sensitive or confidential information.
- Test data provisioning: Provisioning test data to testing environments, such as development, staging, and production environments, using data migration, replication, or synchronization techniques to ensure consistency and integrity across environments.
- Test environment configuration: Configuring testing environments with necessary hardware, software, tools, and resources to simulate real-world conditions and support testing activities effectively.
- Test environment management: Managing test environments throughout the testing lifecycle, including setup, configuration, deployment, maintenance, and decommissioning, to ensure availability, stability, and reliability of testing infrastructure.
- Test environment validation: Validating test environments to ensure they accurately represent production environments, meet testing requirements, and support test execution and analysis effectively.

31. Question: How do you ensure the reliability of automated tests?

Answer: Ensuring the reliability of automated tests requires careful planning, design, implementation, and maintenance of test automation frameworks and test scripts. Key strategies for ensuring the reliability of automated tests include:

- Robust test design: Designing automated tests with clear objectives, well-defined test cases, and reusable test components to ensure reliability, maintainability, and scalability of test scripts.
- Effective error handling: Implementing error handling mechanisms and exception handling routines in test scripts to capture and handle unexpected errors, exceptions, or failures gracefully and prevent test execution from being interrupted or terminated prematurely.
- Synchronization and wait strategies: Using synchronization techniques and wait strategies to ensure that automated tests interact with the application under test (AUT) correctly and wait for expected conditions to be met before proceeding with test execution, avoiding timing-related issues and synchronization errors.
- Logging and reporting: Incorporating logging and reporting mechanisms into test automation frameworks to capture detailed execution logs, screenshots, and error messages for analysis and troubleshooting, facilitating root cause analysis and defect identification.
- Maintenance and version control: Regularly updating and maintaining automated test scripts, frameworks, and dependencies to address changes in the application, environment, or testing requirements, and ensuring compatibility, stability, and reliability of automated tests across different versions and releases.
- Continuous monitoring and validation: Monitoring automated test execution, results, and performance continuously to detect anomalies, inconsistencies, or regressions and validate the reliability, accuracy, and effectiveness of automated tests over time.

32. **Question:** How do you handle flaky tests in test automation?

Answer: Flaky tests are automated tests that produce inconsistent or unreliable results, often due to timing issues, synchronization problems, or environmental factors. Handling flaky tests in test automation requires identifying, analysing, and mitigating the root causes of flakiness to improve test reliability and stability. Key strategies for handling flaky tests include:

- Root cause analysis: Analysing flaky tests to identify underlying causes, such as timing issues, synchronization problems, race conditions, or environmental factors, by reviewing test logs, error messages, and execution traces.
- Test script optimization: Refactoring test scripts to minimize dependencies, reduce complexity, and improve robustness by implementing best practices such as explicit waits, synchronization points, and reliable locators to enhance test reliability and stability.
- Environment isolation: Isolating test environments from external dependencies, fluctuations, or interferences by controlling and stabilizing test environments, configurations, and dependencies to reduce environmental variability and mitigate external factors affecting test execution.
- Retry mechanisms: Implementing retry mechanisms or resilience strategies in test automation frameworks to automatically rerun flaky tests and validate results, tolerating transient failures and mitigating the impact of flakiness on test execution and reporting.
- Failure analysis and triage: Prioritizing and triaging flaky tests based on severity, impact, and frequency to focus efforts on resolving high-priority flaky tests that affect critical functionality or impede test execution, and monitoring and managing low-priority flaky tests to prevent regression and ensure test stability.

33. **Question:** What is the importance of test documentation in software testing?

Answer: Test documentation plays a crucial role in software testing by providing comprehensive documentation of test artifacts, processes, and results throughout the testing lifecycle. Test documentation serves several important purposes:

- Communication: Test documentation serves as a means of communication and collaboration among stakeholders, testers, developers, and project teams by providing clear, concise, and consistent information about testing objectives, requirements, strategies, and results.

- Traceability: Test documentation establishes traceability between test artifacts, requirements, and software components by linking test cases, test scripts, defects, and test results to corresponding requirements, user stories, design documents, and source code, enabling end-to-end traceability and impact analysis.
- Compliance: Test documentation ensures compliance with regulatory standards, industry best practices, and organizational policies by documenting testing activities, methodologies, and results in accordance with established guidelines, standards, and regulations, such as ISO 9000, CMMI, or FDA regulations for medical devices.
- Knowledge transfer: Test documentation facilitates knowledge transfer and knowledge sharing within project teams, organizations, or communities by capturing domain knowledge, testing expertise, and lessons learned from previous projects, enabling reuse, learning, and continuous improvement of testing practices and processes.
- Audit and review: Test documentation provides a basis for audit, review, and evaluation of testing activities, methodologies, and outcomes by stakeholders, quality assurance teams, or external auditors to assess compliance, effectiveness, and efficiency of testing processes and identify areas for improvement.

34. **Question: How do you ensure test coverage for both positive and negative scenarios in test automation?**

Answer: Ensuring test coverage for both positive and negative scenarios in test automation requires a systematic approach to test case design, prioritization, and execution. Key strategies for ensuring comprehensive test coverage include:
- Requirement analysis: Analysing requirements, user stories, and acceptance criteria to identify positive and negative scenarios, boundary conditions, and edge cases that need to be covered by test cases.
- Equivalence partitioning: Partitioning input domains into equivalence classes and designing test cases to cover representative values from each class, including valid and invalid inputs, to ensure coverage of positive and negative scenarios.
- Boundary value analysis: Identifying boundaries and extreme values for input parameters and designing test cases to cover

values at and around boundaries to validate boundary conditions and edge cases for positive and negative scenarios.
- Decision tables: Modelling complex business rules, conditions, and scenarios using decision tables and designing test cases to cover different combinations and permutations of input conditions, decisions, and outcomes to ensure coverage of positive and negative scenarios.
- Error guessing: Leveraging domain knowledge, experience, and intuition to identify potential error-prone areas, vulnerable components, and likely failure modes and designing test cases to deliberately trigger and validate error-handling mechanisms, error messages, and recovery procedures for negative scenarios.

35. **Question: What is the role of risk-based testing in software testing, and how do you implement it?**

Answer: Risk-based testing is an approach to software testing that prioritizes test cases and testing activities based on the level of risk associated with specific functionalities, features, or scenarios. Risk-based testing helps focus testing efforts on high-risk areas that are most likely to contain defects or impact the success of the project. To implement risk-based testing effectively:
- Identify risks: Identify and assess risks associated with the software project, including technical risks, business risks, and operational risks, by conducting risk analysis, brainstorming sessions, and risk identification workshops with stakeholders, domain experts, and project team members.
- Prioritize risks: Prioritize identified risks based on their likelihood of occurrence, potential impact on project objectives, and overall severity using risk matrices, risk registers, or risk scoring techniques to determine which risks require mitigation and testing.
- Define risk-based test strategy: Develop a risk-based test strategy that aligns testing efforts with identified risks, focusing on testing high-risk areas, critical functionalities, and complex scenarios to maximize defect detection and risk mitigation within available resources and constraints.
- Allocate resources: Allocate testing resources, efforts, and timelines based on the prioritized risks and testing objectives, ensuring adequate coverage of high-risk areas and critical

functionalities while balancing the need for thorough testing and timely delivery.
- Monitor and adapt: Continuously monitor and reassess risks throughout the testing lifecycle, adapting testing strategies, priorities, and activities based on changing risk profiles, emerging issues, and feedback from testing activities to ensure that testing efforts remain aligned with project goals and risk mitigation objectives.

36. Question: What are the key considerations for selecting test automation tools?

Answer: Selecting test automation tools requires careful evaluation of various factors, including:
- Compatibility: Ensure that the test automation tool is compatible with the technologies, platforms, frameworks, and environments used in the project, including web, mobile, desktop, API, and database technologies.
- Features: Evaluate the features, capabilities, and functionalities of the test automation tool, such as record and playback, scripting support, object recognition, data-driven testing, keyword-driven testing, and integration with other tools and systems.
- Ease of use: Assess the usability, user interface, and learning curve of the test automation tool to ensure that it is intuitive, user-friendly, and accessible to testers with different skill levels and backgrounds.
- Scalability: Consider the scalability and flexibility of the test automation tool to support testing activities across different projects, teams, and environments, including large-scale, distributed, or complex testing scenarios.
- Maintenance: Evaluate the ease of maintenance, extensibility, and supportability of the test automation tool, including updates, upgrades, compatibility with future releases, and availability of technical support, documentation, and training resources.
- Cost: Consider the total cost of ownership (TCO) of the test automation tool, including licensing fees, subscription costs, maintenance fees, training expenses, and potential costs associated with infrastructure, integration, and scalability.

37. Question: How do you ensure the reliability and stability of automated test execution?

Answer: Ensuring the reliability and stability of automated test execution requires implementing robust test automation practices and techniques, including:

- Environment configuration: Ensure that testing environments are stable, consistent, and properly configured with necessary dependencies, resources, and settings to support automated test execution without interruptions or failures.
- Test data management: Manage test data effectively by ensuring the availability, integrity, and relevance of test data sets, and minimizing dependencies on external data sources or dynamic data that may affect test execution consistency.
- Error handling: Implement error handling mechanisms and exception handling routines in test automation scripts to capture and handle unexpected errors, exceptions, or failures gracefully, and prevent test execution from being interrupted or terminated prematurely.
- Retry strategies: Implement retry mechanisms or resilience strategies in test automation frameworks to automatically rerun failed tests, recover from transient failures, and ensure test execution reliability and stability in dynamic or unstable environments.
- Logging and reporting: Incorporate logging and reporting capabilities into test automation frameworks to capture detailed execution logs, screenshots, and error messages for analysis and troubleshooting, facilitating root cause analysis and defect identification.

38. Question: What is the role of shift-left testing in Agile development?

Answer: Shift-left testing is an approach to software testing that emphasizes early and continuous testing activities throughout the software development lifecycle, starting from the early stages of requirements, design, and development, and shifting testing activities closer to the beginning of the lifecycle. The key role of shift-left testing in Agile development includes:

- Early defect detection: Shift-left testing helps identify defects, errors, and issues early in the development lifecycle, when they

are less costly and easier to fix, by incorporating testing activities such as unit testing, code reviews, and static analysis into the development process.
- Continuous feedback: Shift-left testing enables continuous feedback and collaboration among stakeholders, testers, developers, and customers by providing early visibility into the quality, functionality, and usability of the software, facilitating early course correction, risk mitigation, and requirements validation.
- Reduced cycle time: Shift-left testing accelerates the feedback loop and reduces cycle time by shortening the time between code changes, test execution, and feedback, enabling rapid iterations, incremental development, and faster delivery of high-quality software.
- Improved quality: Shift-left testing improves the overall quality and reliability of the software by integrating testing activities, techniques, and practices into every stage of the development lifecycle, fostering a culture of quality, collaboration, and continuous improvement among the development team.
- Enhanced customer satisfaction: Shift-left testing enhances customer satisfaction by delivering high-quality, defect-free software that meets customer expectations, requirements, and user needs, resulting in improved user experience, loyalty, and business value.

39. Question: What are the key benefits of behaviour-driven development (BDD) for software testing?

Answer: Behaviour-driven development (BDD) is an Agile software development approach that emphasizes collaboration, communication, and shared understanding among stakeholders, developers, and testers to deliver high-quality, customer-centric software. The key benefits of BDD for software testing include:
- Enhanced collaboration: BDD promotes collaboration and communication among stakeholders by using a common language and vocabulary, such as Given-When-Then (GWT) syntax, to describe requirements, acceptance criteria, and test scenarios, fostering shared understanding and alignment of goals and expectations.

- Improved requirements validation: BDD helps validate requirements, user stories, and acceptance criteria by translating them into executable specifications, automated tests, and living documentation that serve as living examples of desired behaviours, facilitating early feedback, clarification, and validation of requirements.
- Automated acceptance testing: BDD enables automated acceptance testing by automating the execution of high-level acceptance tests derived from BDD scenarios, ensuring that the software behaves as intended from an end-user perspective and meets business objectives and user expectations.
- Reduced rework and defects: BDD reduces rework and defects by identifying and addressing misunderstandings, ambiguities, and gaps in requirements early in the development lifecycle, preventing misinterpretations and misalignments that may lead to costly rework, delays, or defects later.
- Increased test coverage: BDD increases test coverage by aligning test scenarios with business goals, user interactions, and system behaviours, ensuring that test cases cover critical functionalities, edge cases, and user workflows that are essential for meeting business objectives and user needs.

40. **Question: What are the key principles of continuous testing in DevOps?**

Answer: Continuous testing is an integral part of DevOps practices that emphasizes early and continuous testing activities throughout the software delivery pipeline to ensure that software changes are tested and validated continuously from development to production. The key principles of continuous testing in DevOps include:
- Shift-left testing: Emphasize early and continuous testing activities from the early stages of development, such as unit testing, integration testing, and API testing, to identify and address defects early in the development lifecycle when they are less costly and easier to fix.
- Test automation: Automate testing activities, processes, and workflows to accelerate test execution, increase coverage, and support continuous integration and delivery (CI/CD) practices, enabling rapid feedback, frequent releases, and faster time-to-market.

- Parallel testing: Perform testing activities in parallel with development and deployment activities to minimize cycle time, reduce bottlenecks, and enable fast, reliable, and repeatable test execution in dynamic and fast-paced DevOps environments.
- Shift-right testing: Extend testing activities beyond development and into production environments by monitoring, analysing, and validating software behaviour, performance, and reliability in real-world conditions to ensure continuous improvement, optimization, and customer satisfaction.
- Feedback-driven development: Leverage feedback from testing activities, user interactions, and production environments to drive continuous improvement, innovation, and optimization of software quality, performance, and user experience throughout the software delivery lifecycle.

41. **Question: What is the importance of test automation in Agile development?**

Answer: Test automation plays a crucial role in Agile development by enabling rapid, reliable, and repeatable testing of software changes and ensuring that quality is maintained throughout the development lifecycle. The importance of test automation in Agile development includes:

- Accelerating feedback: Test automation accelerates feedback by enabling rapid execution of automated tests, providing immediate feedback on code changes, defects, and quality issues to developers, testers, and stakeholders, facilitating early detection and resolution of issues.
- Supporting continuous integration: Test automation supports continuous integration (CI) practices by automating the execution of regression tests, integration tests, and acceptance tests as part of the CI process, ensuring that software changes are tested comprehensively and validated continuously as they are integrated into the codebase.
- Enabling continuous delivery: Test automation enables continuous delivery (CD) practices by automating the validation of software changes, deployment pipelines, and release candidates, ensuring that changes are tested thoroughly and deployed to production quickly and reliably with minimal manual intervention.

- Increasing test coverage: Test automation increases test coverage by automating the execution of a wide range of test cases, scenarios, and workflows across different platforms, devices, and configurations, ensuring comprehensive testing of critical functionalities, edge cases, and user interactions.
- Improving productivity: Test automation improves productivity by reducing manual effort, time, and resources required for test execution, maintenance, and regression testing, allowing testers and developers to focus on higher-value activities such as exploratory testing, test design, and defect analysis.

42. Question: What is the role of continuous integration (CI) in Agile development?

Answer: Continuous integration (CI) is a software development practice that emphasizes frequent integration of code changes, automated testing, and continuous feedback to detect and address integration issues early in the development lifecycle. The role of continuous integration (CI) in Agile development includes:

- Ensuring code quality: Continuous integration ensures code quality by automatically integrating code changes into a shared repository multiple times a day, validating changes through automated tests, and identifying integration issues, compilation errors, or regressions early in the development process.
- Facilitating collaboration: Continuous integration fosters collaboration among developers, testers, and stakeholders by providing a centralized, transparent, and up-to-date codebase, enabling teams to work together, share changes, and resolve conflicts efficiently, reducing coordination overhead and ensuring alignment of goals and objectives.
- Enabling rapid feedback: Continuous integration provides rapid feedback on code changes, build status, and test results to developers, testers, and stakeholders, enabling quick identification and resolution of defects, errors, or issues, and ensuring that software changes are validated and integrated continuously throughout the development lifecycle.
- Supporting automation: Continuous integration supports automation by automating build, test, and deployment processes, enabling teams to automate repetitive tasks, streamline workflows, and accelerate delivery cycles, facilitating continuous

delivery (CD) practices and enabling faster time-to-market for software releases.
- Improving software quality: Continuous integration improves software quality by promoting early detection and resolution of defects, reducing integration risks, and ensuring that software changes are tested, validated, and integrated into the codebase consistently and reliably, resulting in higher-quality, more reliable, and more maintainable software.

43. **Question: How do you ensure test coverage for user interface (UI) testing?**

Answer: Ensuring test coverage for user interface (UI) testing involves designing test cases, scenarios, and workflows that comprehensively validate the functionality, usability, and accessibility of the UI components, features, and interactions. Key strategies for ensuring test coverage for UI testing include:
- Functional testing: Design test cases to verify the correctness and completeness of UI functionality, including user interactions, navigation, input validation, error handling, and data processing, ensuring that the UI behaves as expected and meets functional requirements.
- Usability testing: Evaluate the usability and user experience of the UI by designing test cases to assess navigation, layout, responsiveness, accessibility, readability, and aesthetics, ensuring that the UI is intuitive, user-friendly, and accessible to all users.
- Compatibility testing: Test the UI across different browsers, devices, screen sizes, resolutions, and operating systems to ensure compatibility, consistency, and responsiveness across various platforms and configurations, minimizing rendering issues, layout distortions, or functional discrepancies.
- Performance testing: Assess the performance and responsiveness of the UI under different load levels, network conditions, and usage scenarios to ensure that the UI is fast, responsive, and scalable, minimizing latency, delays, or bottlenecks that may impact user experience.
- Localization testing: Validate the localization and internationalization of the UI by testing UI elements, text labels, messages, and formatting across different languages, cultures,

and locales to ensure linguistic accuracy, cultural relevance, and compliance with regional standards and preferences.

44. **Question: How do you handle test data privacy and security in software testing?**

Answer: Handling test data privacy and security in software testing requires implementing data protection measures, privacy controls, and security practices to safeguard sensitive information and prevent unauthorized access, disclosure, or misuse. Key strategies for handling test data privacy and security include:

- Data anonymization: Anonymize sensitive or personally identifiable information (PII) in test data sets by replacing real data with fictitious or obfuscated data that retains the characteristics and structure of the original data without revealing sensitive information, ensuring privacy and compliance with data protection regulations.
- Data masking: Mask sensitive data elements such as credit card numbers, social security numbers, or email addresses in test environments by replacing real data with masked or encrypted values that preserve format and length while preventing exposure of sensitive information to unauthorized users or systems.
- Data encryption: Encrypt test data during transmission and storage using encryption algorithms and cryptographic techniques to protect data confidentiality, integrity, and authenticity, ensuring that sensitive information remains secure and encrypted throughout testing activities.
- Access controls: Implement access controls, permissions, and authentication mechanisms to restrict access to test data, environments, and systems based on user roles, privileges, and least privilege principles, preventing unauthorized access, tampering, or misuse of test assets.
- Data retention and disposal: Define policies and procedures for data retention and disposal to ensure that test data is retained only for necessary periods and purposes, and securely deleted or anonymized when no longer needed, minimizing data exposure and reducing privacy risks.

45. **Question: How do you handle test case prioritization in Agile development?**

Answer: Handling test case prioritization in Agile development involves assessing the relative importance, risk, and value of test cases and prioritizing them based on criticality, impact, and urgency to ensure that testing efforts are focused on high-priority areas and critical functionalities. Key strategies for handling test case prioritization in Agile development include:

- Risk-based prioritization: Prioritize test cases based on risk factors such as severity, likelihood, and impact of potential defects to focus testing efforts on high-risk areas, critical functionalities, and complex scenarios that are most likely to contain defects or impact project objectives.
- Business value prioritization: Prioritize test cases based on business value, user priorities, and customer needs to ensure that testing efforts align with business objectives, user expectations, and project goals, focusing on features, functionalities, and use cases that deliver the greatest value and impact to stakeholders.
- Requirements-based prioritization: Prioritize test cases based on requirements, user stories, and acceptance criteria to ensure that testing efforts address essential functionalities, behaviours, and acceptance criteria defined for each requirement, prioritizing test cases associated with critical or high-priority requirements.
- Time-based prioritization: Prioritize test cases based on time constraints, deadlines, and project schedules to ensure that testing efforts are aligned with project timelines, release cycles, and delivery milestones, focusing on test cases that can be executed within available timeframes and resources.
- Continuous reassessment: Continuously reassess and reprioritize test cases throughout the Agile development lifecycle based on changing project dynamics, emerging risks, feedback from testing activities, and evolving business priorities to ensure that testing efforts remain aligned with project goals and objectives.

46. **Question:** What are the key considerations for implementing test-driven development (TDD)?

Answer: Implementing test-driven development (TDD) requires careful planning, discipline, and adherence to key principles and practices. Key considerations for implementing TDD include:

- Test-first approach: Adopt a test-first approach by writing automated test cases before implementing production code,

focusing on defining clear, specific, and executable test cases that verify the desired behavior and functionality of the software.
- Red-Green-Refactor cycle: Follow the red-green-refactor cycle of TDD, which involves writing a failing test (red), implementing the minimum code necessary to pass the test (green), and refactoring the code to improve design, readability, and maintainability while keeping all tests passing.
- Incremental development: Embrace incremental development and iterative refinement by writing small, focused tests and implementing small, incremental changes to the codebase, enabling continuous validation, feedback, and improvement of software functionality and design.
- Test coverage and completeness: Ensure comprehensive test coverage and completeness by writing tests for all code paths, edge cases, and requirements, addressing both positive and negative scenarios, and validating different input combinations and boundary conditions to minimize the risk of defects and regressions.
- Refactoring and code quality: Prioritize refactoring and code quality by continuously improving the design, structure, and readability of the codebase, applying design patterns, best practices, and SOLID principles to create clean, maintainable, and extensible code that is easy to understand, modify, and maintain.

47. Question: How do you identify and prioritize test cases for a software application?

Answer: Test cases can be identified and prioritized based on factors such as:
- Business requirements and user stories
- Risk analysis and impact assessment
- Functional and non-functional requirements
- Test coverage goals and objectives
- Complexity and criticality of features
- Historical defect data and usage patterns

Prioritization can be done using techniques such as risk-based testing, requirements-based testing, and value-based testing to focus testing efforts on high-priority areas.

48. Question: What are some common types of software defects, and how do you classify them?

Answer: Common types of software defects include:
- Functional defects: Failures in meeting specified requirements or user expectations.
- Performance defects: Issues related to speed, efficiency, or scalability of the software application.
- Usability defects: Problems with user interface design, navigation, or accessibility.
- Compatibility

49. Question: What is the purpose of a traceability matrix in software testing, and how is it used?

Answer:
- **Purpose of a Traceability Matrix:** A traceability matrix is a document that establishes a mapping between different types of artifacts, such as requirements, test cases, and defects, to ensure that all requirements are covered by test cases and that defects are traced back to their root causes. The purpose of a traceability matrix is to provide visibility into the relationships between requirements, tests, and defects, enabling comprehensive test coverage and effective defect management.
- **Usage of a Traceability Matrix:** A traceability matrix is used to:
  1. Ensure that all requirements are tested: By mapping requirements to test cases, the traceability matrix helps verify that all specified requirements are covered by test cases, ensuring comprehensive test coverage.
  2. Track the status of test cases: The traceability matrix tracks the execution status of test cases and identifies any gaps or missing test coverage for specific requirements.
  3. Trace defects to their root causes: When defects are identified during testing, the traceability matrix helps trace them back to the corresponding requirements and test cases, facilitating root cause analysis and defect resolution.

50. Question: What is boundary value analysis, and how is it used in software testing?

Answer:
- **Boundary Value Analysis (BVA):** Boundary value analysis is a software testing technique used to identify defects and errors at the boundaries of input ranges or conditions. It involves testing

the software application with input values at the boundaries of valid ranges, as well as just above and below those boundaries, to uncover potential issues related to boundary conditions. BVA is based on the principle that defects are more likely to occur at the edges or boundaries of input domains.

- **Usage of BVA:** BVA is used to:
    1. Identify off-by-one errors: By testing input values at the boundaries of valid ranges, BVA helps identify off-by-one errors or inconsistencies in boundary conditions.
    2. Validate input validation logic: BVA validates the correctness of input validation logic by testing input values at the extremes of valid ranges and verifying that the software handles them appropriately.
    3. Improve test coverage: BVA complements other test techniques, such as equivalence partitioning and decision table testing, by providing additional test scenarios and ensuring thorough test coverage of input ranges and conditions.

51. Question: How do you ensure test coverage in both positive and negative scenarios?

Answer:

- **Positive Test Scenarios:** Positive test scenarios focus on verifying that the software behaves as expected when provided with valid inputs and conditions. To ensure test coverage in positive scenarios, testers:
    1. Identify and prioritize positive test cases based on requirements, use cases, and user stories.
    2. Validate expected behaviours, outputs, and system responses against specified requirements and acceptance criteria.
    3. Test different valid input values, boundary conditions, and valid user interactions to ensure comprehensive coverage of positive scenarios.
- **Negative Test Scenarios:** Negative test scenarios focus on verifying that the software handles invalid inputs, error conditions, and edge cases appropriately. To ensure test coverage in negative scenarios, testers:
    1. Identify and prioritize negative test cases based on potential error conditions, boundary values, and invalid inputs.

2. Validate error handling, exception handling, and recovery mechanisms in the software application.
3. Test invalid input values, boundary conditions, and invalid user interactions to simulate real-world usage scenarios and ensure robustness and reliability.

52. Question: What is the difference between load testing and stress testing?

Answer:
- **Load Testing:** Load testing is a type of performance testing that evaluates the behaviour of a software application under normal or expected load conditions. It involves simulating multiple concurrent users or transactions to measure system response times, throughput, and resource utilization. Load testing helps identify performance bottlenecks, scalability issues, and capacity limits under typical usage scenarios.
- **Stress Testing:** Stress testing is a type of performance testing that evaluates the behaviour of a software application under extreme or beyond-normal load conditions. It involves pushing the system to its limits by increasing the load, volume, or intensity of user interactions beyond what it can handle. Stress testing helps identify system weaknesses, stability issues, and failure points under peak load conditions.

53. Question: What is the purpose of regression testing, and how is it different from retesting?

Answer:
- **Regression Testing:** Regression testing is the process of retesting modified or updated software to ensure that existing functionalities have not been affected by changes or enhancements. It aims to verify that previously tested features, functionalities, and behaviours still work as expected after code changes, bug fixes, or system updates. Regression testing helps prevent regressions, validate software stability, and maintain overall system integrity.
- **Retesting:** Retesting is the process of retesting specific defects or issues that were previously identified and reported, typically after they have been fixed or resolved. It focuses on verifying that the reported defects have been correctly addressed and no longer exist in the software application. Retesting ensures that defects

are properly fixed and helps validate the effectiveness of corrective actions.

54. Question: What is the difference between equivalence partitioning and boundary value analysis?
Answer:
- **Equivalence Partitioning:** Equivalence partitioning is a software testing technique that divides the input domain of a software application into classes or partitions of equivalent behavior. Test cases are then selected from each partition to represent the entire class. The goal of equivalence partitioning is to reduce the number of test cases while still ensuring adequate test coverage.
- **Boundary Value Analysis:** Boundary value analysis is a software testing technique that focuses on testing the boundaries or extremes of input ranges or conditions. Test cases are designed to test the minimum and maximum boundaries, as well as just above and below those boundaries. The goal of boundary value analysis is to uncover defects related to boundary conditions, off-by-one errors, and edge cases.

55. Question: What is a defect life cycle, and what are the typical stages?
Answer:
- **Defect Life Cycle:** The defect life cycle, also known as the bug life cycle or issue life cycle, describes the stages that a defect goes through from its identification to its resolution and closure. The typical stages of the defect life cycle include:
    1. **New:** The defect is identified and reported for the first time.
    2. **Open:** The defect is acknowledged by the development team and assigned to a developer for investigation and resolution.
    3. **In Progress:** The developer is actively working on fixing the defect.
    4. **Fixed:** The defect has been fixed by the developer and awaits verification by the testing team.
    5. **Verified:** The fix has been verified by the testing team, and the defect is confirmed to be resolved.
    6. **Closed:** The defect is closed, indicating that it has been successfully resolved and verified.

56. Question: What is risk-based testing, and how is it performed?

Answer:
- **Risk-Based Testing:** Risk-based testing is a software testing approach that focuses on prioritizing testing efforts based on the level of risk associated with different features, functionalities, and components of the software application. It involves identifying, analysing, and assessing risks to determine the most critical areas for testing. Test cases are then prioritized and allocated based on the perceived level of risk, with higher-risk areas receiving greater testing attention.
- **Performing Risk-Based Testing:** Risk-based testing is performed in the following steps:
    1. **Risk Identification:** Identify potential risks, vulnerabilities, and uncertainties associated with the software application, including technical, business, and operational risks.
    2. **Risk Analysis:** Analyse and assess the likelihood and impact of each identified risk on the project objectives, stakeholders, and deliverables.
    3. **Risk Prioritization:** Prioritize risks based on their severity, probability, and potential impact on project success, focusing on high-risk areas that pose the greatest threat.
    4. **Test Planning:** Develop a test strategy and plan that allocates testing resources, efforts, and priorities based on the identified risks and testing objectives.
    5. **Test Execution:** Execute test cases and scenarios targeting high-risk areas, with a focus on risk mitigation, defect prevention, and validation of critical functionalities.

57. **Question: What are the advantages and disadvantages of manual testing?**

Answer:
- **Advantages of Manual Testing:**
    1. **Flexibility:** Manual testing allows testers to adapt test cases dynamically based on their observations, insights, and intuition.
    2. **Exploratory testing:** Manual testing enables exploratory testing, where testers explore the software application without predefined test cases to uncover defects, risks, and usability issues.

3. User perspective: Manual testing allows testers to evaluate the software application from a user's perspective, focusing on usability, accessibility, and user experience.
- **Disadvantages of Manual Testing:**
   1. Time-consuming: Manual testing can be time-consuming, especially for repetitive or large-scale testing efforts, leading to longer testing cycles and delayed releases.
   2. Prone to human errors: Manual testing is susceptible to human errors, inconsistencies, and subjective biases, which may affect the reliability and accuracy of test results.
   3. Limited scalability: Manual testing may not be scalable for complex or high-volume testing requirements, as it relies on human resources and manual effort, which can become inefficient and impractical over time.

58.Question: What are some common challenges faced in software testing, and how do you address them?
Answer:
- **Common Challenges in Software Testing:**
   1. Changing requirements: Testers may encounter challenges due to evolving or unclear requirements, leading to scope creep, ambiguity, and rework.
   2. Resource constraints: Limited time, budget, and resources may pose challenges to testing efforts, impacting test coverage, quality, and thoroughness.
   3. Environment availability: Unavailability or instability of test environments, infrastructure, and dependencies may hinder testing activities and delay testing cycles.
- **Addressing Challenges:**
   1. Clear communication: Effective communication and collaboration between stakeholders, including developers, testers, and project managers, can help clarify requirements, set expectations, and address challenges proactively.
   2. Agile methodologies: Agile practices, such as iterative development, continuous testing, and adaptive planning, can help address changing requirements and promote flexibility and responsiveness in testing.
   3. Test automation: Test automation can help mitigate resource constraints by automating repetitive tasks,

accelerating testing cycles, and improving test coverage and efficiency.

59. Question: How do you ensure traceability between requirements, test cases, and defects?

Answer:
- **Ensuring Traceability:**
    1. **Requirements Traceability:** Trace requirements to test cases by mapping each requirement to one or more corresponding test cases that verify its fulfilment. Use traceability matrices or tools to track the relationship between requirements and test cases throughout the testing process.
    2. **Test Case Execution Traceability:** During test execution, maintain traceability between executed test cases and their corresponding requirements to ensure comprehensive coverage. Record test results, including pass/fail status and defect reports, to track the outcome of each test case.
    3. **Defect Traceability:** Trace defects back to their root causes by linking each reported defect to the test case that identified it, as well as the corresponding requirement it violates. Capture defect-related information, such as severity, priority, and resolution status, to facilitate defect management and tracking.

60. Question: What is a test scenario, and how does it differ from a test case?

Answer:
- **Test Scenario:** A test scenario is a high-level description of a specific user interaction or business process that is to be tested. It defines the sequence of actions, inputs, and expected outcomes for a particular functionality or feature of the software application. Test scenarios are typically derived from user requirements, use cases, and business workflows and serve as the basis for designing detailed test cases.
- **Test Case:** A test case is a detailed set of instructions or steps that specify how to test a particular aspect or behaviour of the software application. It includes preconditions, inputs, actions, expected results, and postconditions for executing a specific test scenario. Test cases are more granular and specific than test

scenarios, providing detailed guidance for testers to follow during test execution.

61. Question: What are some common software testing tools and frameworks?

Answer: Common software testing tools and frameworks include:
- Test management tools: Tools for managing test cases, test plans, test executions, and test results, such as TestRail, HP Quality Centre, and Microsoft Test Manager.
- Test automation tools: Tools for automating test cases and test scripts, such as Selenium, Appium, TestComplete, and Ranorex.
- Performance testing tools: Tools for measuring and analysing the performance and scalability of software applications, such as Apache JMeter, LoadRunner, and Gatling.
- Security testing tools: Tools for identifying and mitigating security vulnerabilities and threats in software applications, such as OWASP ZAP, Burp Suite, and Nessus.
- Continuous integration tools: Tools for automating the build, integration, and deployment of software applications, such as Jenkins, Travis CI, and CircleCI.
- Code coverage tools: Tools for measuring the extent to which source code is executed by test cases, such as Cobertura, JaCoCo, and Istanbul.

62. Question: What is the difference between alpha testing and beta testing?

Answer: Alpha testing and beta testing are two types of user acceptance testing performed to validate software from the end user's perspective:
- Alpha testing: Alpha testing is conducted by a dedicated team of testers within the organization, typically in a controlled environment. It focuses on validating the software's functionality, usability, and performance before it is released to external users.
- Beta testing: Beta testing involves releasing the software to a select group of external users or customers for real-world testing in their own environments. It aims to gather feedback, identify defects, and assess the software's readiness for release based on user acceptance and satisfaction.

63. Question: How do you ensure that software testing is aligned with project objectives and priorities?

Answer: To ensure that software testing is aligned with project objectives and priorities, it is important to:
- Understand the goals, requirements, and constraints of the project, including scope, budget, and timelines.
- Collaborate with stakeholders, including project managers, product owners, and developers, to prioritize testing activities based on project priorities and risks.
- Establish clear testing goals, objectives, and success criteria that align with project objectives and deliverables.
- Continuously monitor and communicate the progress, status, and impact of testing activities on project timelines and milestones.
- Adapt testing strategies and plans based on changes in project scope, requirements, or priorities to ensure that testing efforts remain aligned with project objectives.

64. Question: What is the difference between a defect and a failure?

Answer: In software testing, a defect refers to a flaw, error, or deviation in the software application that may cause it to behave unexpectedly or incorrectly. A defect is typically identified during testing and reported to the development team for resolution. A failure, on the other hand, refers to the manifestation of a defect during the execution of the software application, resulting in incorrect output, behaviour, or performance. While defects exist in the software code, failures occur when those defects are triggered under specific conditions or inputs.

65. Question: How do you measure the quality of software?

Answer: Measuring the quality of software involves using various metrics, indicators, and criteria to assess its attributes and characteristics. Common measures of software quality include:
- Defect density: The number of defects identified per unit of code or functionality.
- Test coverage: The percentage of code or requirements covered by test cases.
- Code complexity: The level of complexity and intricacy of the software code.

- Mean time to failure (MTTF): The average time between software failures or defects.
- Mean time to recovery (MTTR): The average time taken to recover from software failures or defects.
- Customer satisfaction: The level of satisfaction and usability experienced by end users and stakeholders.
- Time to market: The speed and efficiency of delivering software features and updates to the market.

66. Question: What are some common software testing techniques?

Answer: Common software testing techniques include:
- Black-box testing: Testing the functionality of a software application without considering its internal structure or implementation details.
- White-box testing: Testing the internal structure, code, and logic of a software application to ensure completeness and correctness.
- Grey-box testing: Combining elements of both black-box and white-box testing to validate software from both internal and external perspectives.
- Equivalence partitioning: Dividing input data into equivalence classes to reduce the number of test cases required for comprehensive testing.
- Boundary value analysis: Testing input boundaries, limits, and edges to identify defects and errors at the boundaries of valid and invalid ranges.
- Exploratory testing: Freestyle testing approach that involves simultaneous learning, test design, and test execution to uncover defects and risks.
- Regression testing: Testing the software application to ensure that new changes or modifications do not introduce unintended side effects or regressions.

67. Question: How do you ensure that test cases are effective and efficient?

Answer: Ensuring that test cases are effective and efficient involves:
- Designing test cases based on clear, concise, and unambiguous requirements and specifications.

- Writing test cases that cover all possible scenarios, including positive, negative, and edge cases.
- Prioritizing test cases based on risk, criticality, and business impact to focus testing efforts on high-risk areas.
- Reusing test cases where applicable to reduce duplication and improve maintainability.
- Reviewing and validating test cases with stakeholders to ensure accuracy, completeness, and relevance.
- Automating repetitive and routine test cases to improve efficiency and scalability.
- Continuously updating and refining test cases based on feedback, changes in requirements, and lessons learned.

68.Question: What are some common challenges faced in software quality assurance, and how do you address them?

Answer: Common challenges faced in software quality assurance include changing requirements, resource constraints, environment availability, and maintaining test data integrity. These challenges can be addressed by:
- Establishing clear communication and collaboration between stakeholders to address changing requirements effectively.
- Optimizing resource allocation and utilization through effective planning, prioritization, and automation.
- Implementing robust test environment management practices to ensure availability, stability, and consistency of test environments.
- Implementing test data management strategies to maintain the integrity, privacy, and security of test data throughout the testing process.

69.Question: How do you ensure that software requirements are testable and measurable?

Answer: To ensure that software requirements are testable and measurable, it is important to:
- Clearly define requirements using unambiguous language and terminology.
- Break down requirements into smaller, atomic units that can be easily tested.

- Specify acceptance criteria and success criteria for each requirement.
- Ensure that requirements are traceable, meaning that each requirement is linked to one or more test cases that verify its fulfilment.
- Validate requirements with stakeholders to ensure that they are complete, correct, and achievable.

70.Question: What is the role of a software quality assurance engineer?

Answer: The role of a software quality assurance engineer involves:
- Developing and implementing quality assurance processes, procedures, and standards.
- Planning and executing test strategies, test plans, and test cases.
- Conducting functional, non-functional, and regression testing.
- Identifying, documenting, and tracking defects and issues.
- Collaborating with development teams to resolve defects and improve product quality.
- Analysing and reporting test results and quality metrics.
- Participating in reviews, inspections, and audits to ensure compliance with quality standards and requirements.

71.Question: What is the difference between quality assurance and quality control?

Answer: Quality assurance (QA) focuses on preventing defects by implementing processes and procedures to ensure that quality standards are met throughout the software development lifecycle. Quality control (QC), on the other hand, involves detecting and correcting defects through testing, inspections, and reviews. While QA is proactive and preventive, QC is reactive and corrective.

72.Question: What is software quality assurance (SQA), and why is it important?

Answer: Software quality assurance (SQA) is a systematic process of ensuring that software products and processes meet defined quality standards and fulfil user requirements. It involves establishing quality goals, implementing processes and procedures to achieve those goals, and monitoring and evaluating the quality of software throughout the development lifecycle. SQA is important because it helps prevent defects, improves the reliability and performance of software, enhances user satisfaction, and reduces costs associated with rework and defects.

73.Question: What are the key components of a software quality assurance process?

Answer: The key components of a software quality assurance process include:
- Establishing quality goals and objectives.
- Defining quality standards and criteria.
- Developing and implementing quality processes and procedures.
- Conducting reviews, inspections, and audits.
- Performing testing and validation activities.
- Monitoring and measuring quality metrics and indicators.
- Continuously improving quality practices and processes based on feedback and lessons learned.

74.Question: What are the key principles of software quality assurance?
Answer:
- The key principles of software quality assurance include:
    1. Customer focus: Ensuring that software meets the needs and expectations of the customers and stakeholders.
    2. Continuous improvement: Striving for continuous improvement in processes, practices, and outcomes to enhance quality.
    3. Prevention over detection: Emphasizing proactive measures to prevent defects rather than relying solely on defect detection.
    4. Leadership involvement: Leadership commitment and involvement in driving quality initiatives and fostering a culture of quality.
    5. Data-driven decision-making: Using data, metrics, and analytics to make informed decisions and drive quality improvements.
    6. Team collaboration: Promoting collaboration and communication among cross-functional teams to achieve common quality goals.

75.Question: What is the role of risk management in software testing, and how do you prioritize testing activities based on risk?

Answer:
- Risk management plays a crucial role in software testing by identifying, assessing, and mitigating risks that may impact the success of the project.
- Risk-based testing involves prioritizing testing activities based on the likelihood and impact of risks on project objectives and deliverables.
- This includes identifying high-risk areas that pose the greatest threat to project success, such as complex functionalities, critical business processes, or dependencies on external systems.
- Testing efforts are then focused on mitigating these risks through targeted testing and validation activities, such as exploratory testing, boundary testing, and stress testing.

76.Question: How do you ensure that software testing activities are aligned with regulatory requirements and industry standards?

Answer:
- Ensuring that software testing activities are aligned with regulatory requirements and industry standards involves:
    1. Identifying applicable regulations, standards, and guidelines relevant to the software product, industry, and target markets.
    2. Incorporating regulatory and compliance requirements into the testing process, including validation, verification, and documentation.
    3. Conducting risk assessments and gap analyses to identify areas of non-compliance or potential risks to regulatory compliance.
    4. Implementing testing strategies, methodologies, and techniques that address regulatory requirements, such as validation testing, security testing, and compliance testing.
    5. Collaborating with compliance experts, auditors, and regulatory authorities to ensure that testing activities meet the necessary standards and certifications.

77. Question: What strategies do you employ to ensure effective communication between stakeholders during the software testing process?

Answer:
- Effective communication between stakeholders during the software testing process is essential for ensuring alignment, collaboration, and transparency. Strategies to facilitate effective communication include:
    1. Regular status updates and progress reports to keep stakeholders informed about the testing activities, milestones, and outcomes.
    2. Establishing clear channels of communication, such as meetings, emails, and collaboration tools, to facilitate discussions and address issues in a timely manner.
    3. Engaging stakeholders in requirement reviews, test plan discussions, and defect triage meetings to gather feedback, clarify expectations, and resolve discrepancies.
    4. Providing stakeholders with access to testing artifacts, such as test cases, test results, and defect reports, to facilitate visibility and accountability.

78. Question: How do you ensure that software testing efforts are effective and efficient within resource constraints?

Answer:
- Ensuring that software testing efforts are effective and efficient within resource constraints involves:
    - Prioritizing testing activities based on project objectives, risks, and priorities to focus resources on critical areas.
    - Optimizing resource allocation and utilization through effective planning, scheduling, and coordination.
    - Leveraging automation for repetitive and routine testing tasks to improve efficiency and scalability.
    - Conducting risk-based testing to identify high-risk areas that require additional attention and resources.
    - Monitoring and optimizing testing processes, workflows, and tools to minimize waste and maximize productivity.
    - Collaborating with cross-functional teams to leverage expertise, share resources, and align efforts towards common quality goals.

- **79. Question: How do you determine the scope of testing for a software project?**

    Answer: Determining the scope of testing for a software project involves:
    - Analysing project requirements, specifications, and user stories to identify the features and functionalities that need to be tested.
    - Assessing the criticality and complexity of each feature or functionality to prioritize testing efforts.
    - Considering factors such as project timelines, resource constraints, and budget limitations to define the testing scope.
    - Collaborating with stakeholders, including developers, product owners, and end users, to understand their expectations and requirements for testing.
    - Defining the in-scope and out-of-scope items for testing, including any dependencies, interfaces, or integrations that need to be considered.

- **80. Question: What are some common quality assurance methodologies and approaches?**

    Answer: Common quality assurance methodologies and approaches include:
    - Waterfall model: Sequential development process with distinct phases of requirements, design, implementation, testing, and maintenance.
    - Agile methodologies: Iterative and incremental development approaches such as Scrum, Kanban, and Extreme Programming (XP), focusing on adaptive planning, continuous feedback, and collaboration.
    - Lean Six Sigma: Data-driven methodology for improving processes and reducing defects, waste, and variation.
    - Total Quality Management (TQM): Management approach focused on customer satisfaction, continuous improvement, and employee involvement in quality initiatives.

www.ingramcontent.com/pod-product-compliance
Lightning Source LLC
Chambersburg PA
CBHW070947220526
45471CB00007B/2928